Original title:
The Green Glow

Copyright © 2025 Creative Arts Management OÜ
All rights reserved.

Author: Juliette Kensington
ISBN HARDBACK: 978-1-80581-866-3
ISBN PAPERBACK: 978-1-80581-393-4
ISBN EBOOK: 978-1-80581-866-3

Glimmering Canopy

In the forest, lights abound,
Flickering laughter all around.
Trees wear glitter like a crown,
As squirrels dance without a frown.

Fireflies cha-cha in the night,
With tiny shoes, oh what a sight!
A raccoon dons a flashy coat,
While leaping frogs play the float.

Bioluminescent Dreams

A toadstool wears a neon hat,
With polka dots and a friendly chat.
Glowworms giggle on the floor,
As crickets play the piano score.

Bubbly moss sings in the breeze,
As chipmunks do as they please.
"Jump and wiggle, hop and wiggle!"
They rhyme along with glee and giggle.

Aurora of the Foliage

Mushrooms blush in cosmic hues,
While raccoons strut in party shoes.
The leaves hum tunes of witty lore,
While owls make puns till we adore.

Glow sticks tumble, twirl, and rise,
In this wacky world, so full of guise.
With every glow comes a silly jest,
Nature's humor is quite the zest.

Shimmering Moss

Mossy carpets spark with cheer,
As frogs kick back and sip their beer.
The slugs slide in their shiny suits,
While beetles shake their tiny boots.

A laughing brook throws bubbles high,
As butterflies wiggle and sigh.
Witty whispers in the glade,
In this disco, fun is made.

Whispers of Radiant Flora

In the garden, critters dance,
A frog in tights, what a chance!
The daisies giggle, swaying light,
As fireflies join the silly fight.

Worms are wearing hats so grand,
They groove and twirl to a band.
A ladybug plays a tiny drum,
While mushrooms jiggle, feeling numb.

The sun peeks in with a chuckle,
As squirrels juggle acorns and muckle.
Bouncing bees with striped attire,
Buzz tunes that lift you even higher.

All the trees are rolling their eyes,
At dancing shrubs, what a surprise!
Nature's laughter fills the air,
In this boom, none have a care!

Gleaming Groves

In the woods, the bright ones shine,
Gnarled roots twist and intertwine.
A raccoon wears spectacles wide,
As wise owls look on, full of pride.

The hedgehogs play a game of tag,
While rabbits hop with a hearty brag.
Twinkling leaves in playful tease,
Swirling in winds that twist like breeze.

A chipmunk with a cheeky grin,
Hoarding snacks for a bash to begin.
The breeze whispers secrets so dear,
While branches giggle, drawing near.

Dancing shadows in rays so bold,
The grove's antics never grow old.
A parade of critters in a row,
Under the beams of a sunny glow!

The Lanterns of Nature

Beneath the stars, a party's set,
With lanterns swaying, you can bet.
Fireflies twirp and they shimmer bright,
As crickets chirp their tunes at night.

The owls swoop low in fancy hats,
While raccoons spin in jazzy chats.
Pine cones roll with mischief so grand,
As all join in, hand in hand.

Glowworms strut, so proud, so bold,
In this forest, laughter unfolds.
Silly gales that tickle and tease,
As treetops sway in dancing feeze.

Jellybeans dot the forest floor,
As chipmunks bicker over the score.
With every twinkle, joy ignites,
In this whimsical world of delights!

Illuminated Canopy

Underneath this leafy dome,
A kingdom buzzing, all feel at home.
Grass blades giggle, wriggling low,
While ants parade, putting on a show.

Canopies of laughter spin,
With leads of vines, they dance and grin.
The squirrels drop their nuts with flair,
As they leap around without a care.

A snail with shades slides on the trail,
While butterflies gossip, tell a tale.
This forest buzzes with glee and grace,
In the quirky rhythms of nature's space.

Glowing ferns with radiance flash,
As nighttime animals begin to clash.
Twinkling stars join in the fun,
Beneath the great canopy, everyone!

Tranquil Glimmer of Leaves

In the woods, leaves dance and jig,
Squirrels sneer, plotting a gig.
Moss hides secrets, winks, and grins,
As raccoons watch, with cheeky spins.

Amidst the branches, shadows play,
Trees gossip loudly, 'What a day!'
A playful breeze teases the boughs,
Nature's jesters take plenty of bows.

The sun peeks through, just to tease,
Lighting up tricks on buzzing bees.
A butterfly trips in splendor bright,
Landing on noses, pure delight!

So wander here, let worries float,
Amongst the giggles, keep your coat.
For laughter lives where green things bend,
Nature's humor will never end.

Nature's Shimmering Soul

In the garden, gnomes all chat,
Wearing hats both big and fat.
Worms play poker in the clay,
While bees buzz loud, 'Just one more play!'

The daisies gossip, petals aflame,
Competing hard for garden fame.
A chatty toad croaks out a pun,
While sunflowers stretch and soak up fun.

Loopy vines reach out for style,
Tripping up a passing child.
With giggles and sneezes, flowers bloom,
Nature's laughter fills every room.

So prance around in joyous spree,
Nature's soul is wild and free.
Join the fun where green things thrive,
And find the jokes that come alive!

Whispers of the Emerald Visitant

In the meadow, guests arrive,
A spotted bug plays hide and jive.
Crickets chirp a catchy beat,
While ants march on, oh so neat.

The timid frogs, they sing a tune,
Beneath the bright and laughing moon.
Fireflies waltz in a glowing race,
And tumbleweeds share a funny face.

Chatty flowers lean to hear,
The latest gossip, loud and clear.
A dandelion dreams of flight,
Spinning tales on a starry night.

So join the fun, just let it flow,
In nature's world, we steal the show.
With every rustle, every grin,
A spark of joy where laughter's been.

Luminous Wilderness

In the wild, the shadows spin,
Where creatures plot and giggle in.
A bushy tail whips round in glee,
While owls wink, 'Come play with me!'

The streams are bubbling, full of cheer,
Sending splashes far and near.
A playful otter slides right past,
In a race to see who's the fastest.

The sun sets low, igniting tricks,
As crickets set up their music licks.
Branches sway, a comical sight,
As creatures gather for the night.

So come along and join the spree,
In laughing woods, you're wild and free.
In every rustle, dance and prance,
Discover joy in nature's dance!

Shimmering Petals

In the garden, petals shine,
Bees are buzzing, feeling fine.
Butterflies dance with a grin,
Chasing shadows, round they spin.

Laughter echoes, dogs run wild,
A cat lounges, oh so styled.
Sunflowers wink, saying "hello,"
While ants march in a funny row.

A frog croaks jokes from the pond,
Tadpoles giggle, of which they're fond.
The branches sway, can you believe?
Nature's party, no one can leave.

At dusk, the colors start to fade,
Fireflies twinkle, a glow parade.
With each flicker, a joke is tossed,
In this world, no fun is lost.

Nature's Illustrated Light

A squirrel dressed in vibrant hues,
Stealing berries, he can't refuse.
Down the path, he hops with flair,
In his backpack, snacks to share.

The birds are singing silly tunes,
Flipping leaves, they dance like loons.
Worms tailgate, all lined in rows,
While the flowers strike their poses.

The sun peeks through the leafy trees,
Tickling roots and dancing leaves.
With friends around, they laugh and play,
Holding onto sunlight's sway.

When evening falls, the stars appear,
Twinkling laughs that we all hear.
Nature's book is filled with cheer,
As we share stories, far and near.

Glowing Moss

Underfoot, moss looks so bright,
A carpet green, what a sight!
Frogs leap out with a little croak,
Wishing to join the nature spoke.

The mushrooms giggle, quite absurd,
In polka dots, they share a word.
A toadstool sings a silly rhyme,
In this place, there's no such time.

Here, every stone's a jester's hat,
Rolling downhill, oh what a spat!
As lizards lounge in sunlight's gleam,
Giggling softly, it's more than a dream.

And when the moon begins to rise,
The fireflies dance with tiny pies.
"Catch me if you can," they jest,
In this glowing shade, we feel the best.

Iridescent Meadow

In the meadow, colors burst,
With every step, we quench our thirst.
Grasshoppers hop with a funny bounce,
As daisies giggle in their flounce.

A rabbit wears a floppy hat,
With a sign that says, "Look at that!"
Gather around for a silly tale,
Of the day a snail set sail.

Clouds drift by, wearing smiles,
Chasing sunbeams for a while.
Bumblebees slide on dew-wet clover,
Winking at us, feeling bolder.

Evening falls, the stars ignite,
A sky of giggles, pure delight.
In this meadow, laughter's shared,
With every glow, no heart's impaired.

Ferns of Florid Light

In a jungle, ferns do sway,
Wishing for a brighter day.
They giggle when the sun's too bright,
Wearing shades that fit just right.

A squirrel slips, oh what a sight,
Dancing on a branch, oh so light.
With laughter ringing all around,
In this green stage, joy is found.

Dappled Light of Life

Beneath the trees, the shadows tease,
A sunbeam smiles with playful ease.
Frogs in booties jump and prance,
While ladybugs join in the dance.

Dancing mushrooms sway with flair,
Whispering secrets to the air.
Squirrels wear their acorn hats,
As laughter echoes, 'Oh, look at that!'

Sparkling Sprouts

Tiny sprouts with mustache leaves,
Giggling at the world, oh please!
Wiggling worms in party style,
Shaking roots and dancing wild.

In this green patch, no one frets,
All join in, no regrets.
The snails slide by with loads of cheer,
In their shells, they hold a beer!

Summer's Incandescent Touch

Summer days are full of cheer,
Sunny rays make shadows clear.
Grasshoppers jump in silly play,
Wishing every day's a stay.

Bees buzz by with jokes to share,
In this garden, joy's everywhere.
Flowers giggle, swaying slow,
In this calm, we steal the show.

Moonlit Foliage

In shadows thick, where laughter hides,
The leaves dance funny, no one abides.
A raccoon struts in a top hat grand,
Twirling his tail, isn't life just planned?

The owls hoot jokes, perched on a limb,
While crickets chirp their night-time hymn.
A squirrel laughs, with nuts to share,
In this leafy circus, all have flair.

Warmth Within Green Haze

In jungles dense where giggles sway,
The ferns whisper secrets in a play.
The vines, they tease the wandering feet,
"Step here, my friend! You'll have a treat!"

A turtle's shell is a disco ball,
Reflecting light, making shadows crawl.
Frogs in tuxedos croak a refrain,
"Join the fun, it'll drive you insane!"

A Symphony of Green Light

Conducted by sprites with wands of glee,
The orchestra's played by a buzzing bee.
A jolly toad takes the lead with flair,
   Singing the tune that fills the air.

Worms play banjos beneath the ground,
While branches sway to the gentle sound.
Laughter ripples through leaves on high,
   In this happy concert, oh my, oh my!

Ethereal Tints of Nature

Amidst the hues where giggles blend,
A chameleon jokes, he's hard to offend.
With colors that shift in the sun's bright sheen,
He turns into pink, quite the routine!

Sunflowers grin, their petals aglow,
Sharing the gossip none seem to know.
The breeze carries chuckles from flower to tree,
In this vibrant realm, all are carefree.

Glorious Flora

In a garden where daisies dance,
A butterfly slips in a clumsy prance.
Flowers giggle, their laughter loud,
As a snail takes on the role of proud.

Leafy wigs on every stem,
A frog wearing a tiara, a true gem.
Caterpillars doing the cha-cha slide,
While bees buzz around, their pollen pride.

Sunflowers peek with a golden grin,
Tickled by winds, they sway and spin.
Worms cracking jokes in the soft brown bed,
While ants form chains like they're being led.

Roses blushing with mischief bright,
Under the glowing orb of light.
Every petal a story, a laugh to share,
In this botanical comedy, beyond compare.

Myth in the Moss

A fairy sneezed on a mushroom high,
The gnome nearby let out a sigh.
Mossy carpets gleamed with mirth,
Chasing mushrooms for all they're worth.

Underground, the roots did cheer,
As a rabbit waltzed without any fear.
Moss all a-sway, like a dancing crowd,
With a chorus of giggles, oh so loud.

Lichens whispered secrets so sly,
While crickets chirped a lullaby.
In this verdant realm, odd tales arise,
Like frogs in tuxedos, oh what a surprise.

In shadows thick and laughter bold,
Stories of mossy magic unfold.
With chuckles echoing through the grove,
Who knew such mischief could live and rove?

Enigma of the Green

A riddle wrapped in leafy shrouds,
Dancing shadows, they gather crowds.
What's green and giggles, a puzzling sight?
A wobbly lettuce in the fading light.

A bouncing pea, with a hat askew,
Looking for a partner, oh what to do?
The grass tickles toes as it sways,
In the vibrant theater of nature's play.

Dandelions join with humorous flair,
As weeds sprout tales beyond compare.
A carpet of clover, a puzzle vast,\nWhere every laugh leaves the moments cast.

Whispers in leaves, a flicker of cheer,
With secrets so silly, ever near.
In this enigma where giggles dwell,
Nature's a jokester, can't you tell?

Verdure's Embrace

Wrapped in green, what a sight to behold,
A cucumber wearing sunglasses, oh so bold.
Kale is cracking jokes with a twirl,
While spinach twinkles, giving a whirl.

Broccoli struts in a broccoli ballet,
As carrots giggle, "Let's seize the day!"
Herbs whisper poems in the sun's bright glow,
While peas in pods trade gossip, oh what a show!

A hopscotch path made from daisies fair,
Mushrooms peek in, with chubby flair.
The vines intertwine, a cuddly embrace,
In verdant laughter, they find their place.

So here in the garden, where fun takes flight,
Every leaf a comedian in the warm daylight.
In verdure's arms, laughter's the key,
To unlock the secrets of nature's decree.

Celestial Greenery

In the garden, plants conspire,
Whispering secrets, they never tire.
Frogs wear hats, all in a row,
Looking dapper in the verdant glow.

Worms having tea with butterflies,
Chatting about the bright blue skies.
Lettuce doing a wiggly dance,
Caught in the sun's silly romance.

The flowers giggle, sharing jokes,
Poking fun at the sleepy blokes.
With a glittering, shimmering gleam,
They're living out a leafy dream.

All under the sun's playful stare,
Nature's humor hangs in the air.
Where veggies wear socks, and tall weeds sway,
Making the most of their silly play.

Elysian Fields Aglow

In meadows filled with sparkling sights,
Daisies toast to their hilarious nights.
Bumblebees break-dance, don't you see?
While ants host a wild jamboree.

The sunflowers wave, their heads held high,
Telling corny jokes that make you sigh.
With petals like umbrellas, oh so grand,
They shelter the ants from a soft, sweet band.

Under the moon, the crickets cheer,
While fireflies flash like they're in a leer.
Jumping around in the glowing scene,
With laughter echoing through all the green.

As twilight falls, the fun won't stop,
With all of nature ready to hop.
In fields of light, they'll dance till dawn,
And make sure daybreak comes with a yawn.

Phosphorescent Blooms

In the twilight, flowers start to giggle,
With petals that seem to dance and wiggle.
A daffodil laughs, a rose cracks a pun,
Under the watch of the chuckling sun.

Lilies whisper secrets to the night,
About tall tales, and what feels right.
The violets snicker, rolling on the ground,
While dandelions drift, a merry sound.

Bright pumpkins join in with glee and cheer,
With a squash that smiled, "What's up, dear?"
They play hopscotch on a vine-lined path,
Creating a maze of botanical math.

Each bloom in the garden shares a tale,
Of hiccups and stumbles, without fail.
Together they flourish, they twirl and play,
Adding laughter to the end of the day.

Light Amongst Ivy

Under the ivy, chuckles arise,
As squirrels debate the best disguise.
"Is my acorn hat too big?" one sighs,
While the others just roll their eyes.

The shadows wiggle, casting a prank,
As birds throw a party, filled with banter rank.
Caterpillars giggle, plotting their flight,
Wishing to join in the comedy night.

Twinkling lights dance on leaves all around,
As the forest floor resonates with sound.
A wiggly worm joins, makes all cheer,
In this leafy circus, there's nothing to fear.

With laughter aplenty and joy unlimited,
Nature's fun spirit can't be omitted.
From blossoms of cheer to whispers of glee,
Every moment vibrates with pure jubilee.

Glow of Nature's Canvas

In the forest where shadows play,
Creatures giggle in bright array.
Leaves wearing hats of vibrant flair,
Dance to the rhythm, without a care.

Butterflies wink in a swirling spree,
While bees buzz jokes, as happy as can be.
A squirrel slips on a mossy heel,
And the mushrooms chuckle at every meal.

The sun paints smiles on every tree,
With whispers of joy, so silly and free.
Nature's laughter fills the air,
A canvas of whimsy, beyond compare.

As night falls, all creatures align,
Sharing secrets over dandelion wine.
And stars shine down with a twinkling cheer,
Nature's canvas glows bright, full of beer!

Sunkissed Leprechaun's Path

On a stroll through fields kissed by light,
A leprechaun giggles, what a sight!
He dances with daisies, bright and bold,
Spreading laughter before he folds.

With pockets of gold, he plays peek-a-boo,
Tickling the daisies, thrilling them too.
'Join me for tea, it's brewed in a shoe,'
He chuckles and twirls, as they laugh anew.

Bouncing on rainbows, tossing out jests,
He tells tales of trolls and opportunist pests.
The wind whispers gossip, soft and light,
As the leprechaun's giggles take flight.

At dusk, he slips into slimy green streams,
Where frogs break the silence with hiccupped dreams.
And as the moon shimmers with playful mirth,
The leprechaun's laughter fills up the earth!

Soft Glows in the Thicket

In the thicket, a ruckus brews,
A crew of raccoons in party shoes.
They disco on logs, oh what a sight,
With fireflies flashing like disco light.

A hedgehog spins with a twist so neat,
While owls bob their heads to the beat.
Crickets crackle with comedic flair,
In this thicket, there's laughter to spare.

'Hey there, badger! Show us your dance!'
He shimmies and shakes, given the chance.
A fox rolls in, wearing shades of blue,
Says, 'Is this a party? Well, I'll join too!'

As night deepens, the giggles grow wild,
In the thicket, nature's joy unfiled.
With soft glows shining, the fun's in full swing,
Every critter's out for a hoot and a fling!

Envious Glade

In a glade so fine, with laughter so dear,
Trees make comparisons, drawing near.
'Look at my leaves!' one tree does boast,
While others chuckle, raising a toast.

With vines that wiggle and branches that sway,
The flowers conspire to brighten the day.
'Why are they so bright?' a thorn prickles out,
'It's because we have fun, there's never a doubt!'

The mushroom jokes are a hit of the feast,
While ladybugs laugh, not fearing the beast.
With whispers of envy, but joy intertwined,
In this glade of laughter, all woes left behind.

As day takes a bow, the moon starts to rise,
With twinkling stars, lighting up their skies.
In the envious glade, they dance with a plan,
Spreading joy with each laugh, just like they can!

Garden of Glowing Secrets

In the garden where gnomes dance,
With glowworms sporting a funny prance.
They tickle the hedgehogs with their light,
While daisies giggle with sheer delight.

A frog in a hat croaks a tune,
Under the watch of a smiling moon.
The flowers burst out into laughter,
As a snail races, seeking ever after.

Bugs compete in a wobbly race,
While squirrels gather for a nutty chase.
The carrots wink with their leafy hats,
As playful shadows chase the spry little rats.

In this glow, secrets twirl and spin,
Where laughter begins and daylight's thin.
The garden laughs with whispers sweet,
In its bubbling joy, none can compete.

Illumined Canopy

Under the trees where bright things peek,
The squirrels chatter, so sly and cheek.
With glimmers of mischief in their eyes,
They mock the owls as wisdom flies.

At night the branches begin to giggle,
As fireflies dance and play a wiggle.
The leaves chuckle with rustling sound,
While moonbeams make their rounds all around.

Raccoons wear masks for their late-night spree,
Raiding picnics, oh what a sight to see!
They tumble and trip, what a silly crew,
As laughter echoes in the forest hue.

The canopy glows in laughter's embrace,
As nature's jesters put on a race.
With crazy antics and silly sights,
The forest gleams with vibrant delights.

Glimmering Sylvan Grove

In the grove where the shadows giggle,
Dance a band of frogs, each one a wiggle.
With each leap, they pop like confetti,
Their antics leave the trees quite petty.

The mushrooms sport funny little hats,
While twirling around with chattering bats.
A hedgehog juggles acorns with flair,
And the wise old owl just stops to stare.

A rabbit slips in sparkling shoes,
As the breeze whispers silly news.
The leaves quiver with equal parts fun,
While everyone joins in, no one's outdone.

While the glow from the bugs adds to the jest,
Even the nightingale takes a rest.
In this grove of giggles, they all know,
Life's a party, with a perfect glow.

Celestial Leafy Whisper

In the whispers of leaves, secrets hide,
Each twig is a comedian, full of pride.
With chuckles that tickle the stars above,
And echoes of laughter that sprout from love.

A chipmunk plays tricks on his friends,
As mischievous nibbles are what he sends.
The branches sway as if in a dance,
In this nighttime banquet, everyone has a chance.

Crickets play tunes that make you laugh,
While skunks wear shirts, oh, what a gaffe!
The moon beams down with a giggling face,
Enjoying the chaos of this leafy place.

With glimmers of joy in this soft, green hue,
The forest rejoices, clean and new.
In the playful winks of the night so bright,
All creatures unite for a whimsical flight.

Green Reverie

In a field of peas, the rabbits dance,
Wearing tiny hats, they prance and prance.
Lettuce leaves flutter, waving with glee,
While carrots chuckle, oh what a spree!

A frog in a top hat tries to sing,
But slips on a snail, what a funny thing!
The daisies giggle, they can't hold back,
As the clumsy frog wobbles off track.

Ants form a train on a sugar trail,
While a lazy snail is chasing a snail.
The garden's alive with chuckles and cheer,
As the frolicking creatures spread laughter near.

Aglow in the Grove

A squirrel in shades sits sipping his tea,
While fireflies wink, planning a spree.
Mushrooms wear hats, all painted bright,
As they throw a party beneath the moonlight.

The trees tell jokes that tickle the bark,
As owls recite tales till it's way past dark.
The raccoons perform with a sparkle and flair,
Making the night feel like a fair!

A hedgehog attempts to play the guitar,
But strums on his spikes, oh what a bizarre!
The laughter erupts, it's a real hoot,
Under the glow, all feel quite cute.

Where Leaves Glimmer

In the heart of the park, where the leaves shine bright,
A parrot paints rainbows in the soft twilight.
Bouncing beetles duel with gleaming delight,
While a caterpillar struts with all its might.

A duck in a bowtie steals bread from the ducks,
They waddle around, all in muddled trucks.
The trees are giggling, what a sight to behold,
As critters and chuckles together unfold.

A raccoon juggles acorns in style,
While the bushes sway and twist with a smile.
Nature's grand circus, under the light's shimmer,
Where laughter and fun will never grow dimmer.

Subtle Blossoms Bright

In the garden of quirks, the flowers do sway,
Whispering secrets in a humorous way.
The tulips are gossiping over a plot,
While daisies compare the best sun to spot.

A bee in a tuxedo flits here and there,
Trying to charm all, with his sweet, silly flair.
The petunias snicker, oh such a show,
As giggling blossoms put on a glow.

With bumblebees buzzing a tune quite absurd,
A ladybug hums, singing each word.
Together they spread joy, oh what a sight,
In a patch full of giggles, all feeling just right.

Sparkling Green Trails

In the forest, a shimmer's found,
Shimmery critters bounce all around.
Frogs in tuxedos, ready to dance,
Wobble and giggle, they take their chance.

Mossy carpets, a soft, green bed,
Squirrels in pajamas, not one's misled.
Chasing their tails with a squeaky cheer,
In this wild party, there's no room for fear.

Glowing confetti made of clover,
Escaping from ants, oh they're in trouble!
Bottle cap hats on beetles in flight,
Wobbling sideways, what a silly sight!

So come join the laughter, don't miss your cue,
With giggly friends, there's fun to pursue!
Nature's a comical, wild, joyful place,
Come twirl with the green and share in the grace.

Leafy Luminescence

Under the canopy, leaves wear a grin,
Dancing like mad in the gentle wind.
A mouse in a hat offers cheese with a wink,
While turtles in shades just lounge by the sink.

The flowers gossip in colors so bright,
Trading their secrets as day turns to night.
A dandelion puffs, its wish to the sky,
While butterflies chuckle, floating by.

Glowing fireflies join in the fun,
Playing tag 'til the day is done.
The breeze brings a joke, a soft, subtle tease,
As critters in chorus just laugh with ease.

So leap in the laughter, let go of your woes,
In leafy laugh-fests, silliness grows!
With nature's giggles lighting the scene,
Join the party, feel the gleam!

Gentle Glow of Nature

A shimmer on petals, a soft little laugh,
As daisies receive it, a gleeful autograph.
Bumblebees buzzing with joy in the air,
In striped little outfits, they dance without care.

The brook sings a tune, a bubbling delight,
While rocks play the drums, oh what a sight!
A squirrel jokes, "I'm winning the race!"
As hedgehogs roll in, just saving their space.

Starlight tickles the leaves' leafy skin,
Whispers of laughter, where did it begin?
And in the moon's glow, the woods feel alive,
Critters unite, and the silliness thrives.

So gather your friends, both furry and small,
Join laughter's adventure, let giggles enthrall!
The gentle joys here will spin you around,
In nature's warm laughter, pure fun will abound.

Resplendent Green Echoes

In the thicket, a flurry of green,
A raccoon in tights, quite the scene!
"Look at me dance!" he shouts with glee,
As rabbits join in for the jubilee.

Glowworms hum tunes in sync and in style,
Mice tap their feet, stay awhile!
Pinecones roll in, get swept off their feet,
Nature's cute concert, oh what a feat!

Laughter erupts from behind a tall tree,
Where a gopher claims victory on a spree.
"Mushrooms are mushrooms, but who's the best?"
With fungi hopping, they start the jest!

So chuckle with critters, let joy be the call,
In echoes of green, come one, come all!
The nature of fun is a sight you should seek,
With giggles aplenty and laughter unique!

Forest's Soft Enlightenment

In the woods, a squirrel beams,
Wearing shades and sipping creams.
Mushrooms dance with silly grace,
Trees giggle in their leafy space.

Frogs croak jokes, a funny show,
While woodland critters steal the flow.
A raccoon with a snack so grand,
Shares it with a talking hand.

Sunlight flickers, making fun,
Of shadows that chase everyone.
A dancing patch, so bright and bold,
Teases ants, like tales retold.

In this forest, laughter reigns,
Where even twigs have funny veins.
So join the whimsy, don't be shy,
In the woods, we live and fly.

Glade of Light

In the meadow, bees behave,
With tiny suits, so chic and brave.
Flowers giggle, petals twirl,
As butterflies around them swirl.

A jester toad, quite out of place,
Springs around with funny grace.
He slips and trips, but no one mind,
In this glade, true joy you'll find.

The sunlight's laughter sparkles bright,
Tickling shadows, pure delight.
A picnic feast for all to share,
Even the ants run with flair!

In this place, worry takes flight,
And laughter fills the heart with light.
Join the fun, don't miss the chance,
In the glade, come join the dance!

Mystic Emerald Gaze

In a glen where giggles grow,
A wise old owl steals the show.
"Whooo's the funniest?" he asks in glee,
As chattering rabbits plead, "It's me!"

A leafy hat on a chipmunk's head,
Bounces joyfully, with words unsaid.
A stream laughs with a bubbly sound,
As pebbles giggle, scattered 'round.

Mossy carpets tell old jokes,
While forest creatures sip their cokes.
The sun hides behind a fluffy cloud,
As everyone sings, so loud and proud.

In this mystical space divine,
Laughter lingers, sunshine shines.
Join the party, dance along,
In emerald hues, you can't go wrong!

Ethereal Green

Amidst the leaves of vibrant hue,
Lies a ladybug with a funny view.
She spins around, a ballet grand,
While caterpillars cheer and stand.

Grasshoppers host a hopping race,
With tiny hats, a silly chase.
The winner toasts with dewdrop cheer,
While flowers giggle, "Bring us beer!"

Fuzzy bees buzz with a tune,
While dancing with a friendly raccoon.
In this realm of laughter and dream,
Life's a party, or so it seems.

Join the revelry, lose your frown,
In ethereal shades, let joy abound.
For here in this leafy, lush retreat,
Life and laughter are truly sweet!

Vibrant Shadows

In a garden of giggles, the shadows play,
They dance with the daisies in a bright ballet.
A frog wears a crown, all regal and proud,
While the sun's tickled rays make the daisies bow.

A squirrel juggling acorns, so flashy and spry,
Tells jokes to the flowers, oh me, oh my!
The butterflies chuckle, they flutter with glee,
As the shadows twist funny shapes on the lea.

With whispers of mischief, the leaves take their turn,
Tickling the branches, a raucous to learn.
While grasshoppers sing, all serenely offbeat,
The shadows keep laughing, they cannot be beat.

So join in the frolic, let laughter ensue,
As shadows and flowers play peek-a-boo.
With a splash of absurdity, nature's best show,
In a world full of colors, not just black and snow.

Celestial Fern

In the woods, there's a fern, so quirky and spry,
It wears tiny glasses and winks with one eye.
With leaves that are laughing, a ticklish delight,
It tells all the secrets of day turning night.

A snail with a hat that's far too big fits,
Sips tea with the mushrooms, exchanging some wits.
The stars join the laughter, they twinkle and glow,
As the fern spins its tales in a whimsical flow.

With mushrooms in polka dots leaving their beds,
They dance in the moonlight, atop squirrel-heads.
While frogs croak their choruses, off-key but proud,
Even crickets join in, creating a crowd.

So tread softly, dear friend, in the night's velvet balm,
Where the fern spins its stories, both silly and calm.
In a universe filled with giggles and grace,
You'll find laughter unfurling in this leafy space.

Verdant Echoes

In the heart of the meadow, laughter resounds,
As daisies debate who's the fairest in towns.
A chorus of crickets joins in with a cheer,
While a rabbit with glasses reads gossip, oh dear!

The trees whisper secrets, their branches all sway,
As the wind throws a party with leaves in the fray.
The echoes of chuckles bounce off the deer,
Who prance to the rhythm, their faces sincere.

With sprouts wearing shoes, all laced up too tight,
They trip on the clovers, oh what a sight!
The sun peeks through giggles and chuckles galore,
In this place where the echoes make spirits soar.

So gather your friends and run wild in the grass,
In a verdant venue where good times amass.
With each giggle and whisper, the world finds its tone,
In a landscape of joy where the heart feels at home.

Luminescent Foliate

In a forest of twinkles where the leaves gently dance,
The ferns wear their hats, giving laughter a chance.
A raccoon in pajamas steals cookies, oh wow!
While the fireflies flash, 'Let's have fun right now!'

Beneath the bright moon, the owls hoot in jest,
While the frogs form a band, in their Sunday best.
The foliage chuckles, its secrets unfurl,
As mischief and magic paint the night's swirl.

With a troupe of wild beets doing pirouettes,
And a snail who recites all the best internet pets.
The laughter grows louder, like whispers of cheer,
In a carnival of colors, with giggles near.

So skip through the night, let the silliness flow,
In this luminescent realm where the weirdos all glow.
With the fables of foliage and jokes in the air,
It's a playful assembly, no worries or care.

Enchanted by Chlorophyll

In a garden full of leaves,
Dancing bugs in happy eaves.
Lettuce wears a leafy frown,
While carrots sway up and down.

Silly squirrels plot and scheme,
To steal a cabbage dream.
Pickles giggle on the vine,
As garden gnomes sip on brine.

Radiance in the Underbrush

Frogs in tuxedos sing tonight,
Underneath the moon's soft light.
Flowers gossip, petals sway,
While mushrooms join the cabaret.

Bumblebees with tiny hats,
Dance around like chubby cats.
Dandelions cheer and shout,
As crickets leap and bop about.

Light of the Forest Veil

Beneath the trees, a waltz begins,
With twirling ferns and joyful spins.
Squirrels wheelbarrow through the grass,
While vines hang on, just like lass.

A hedgehog rolls, it's quite a sight,
As fireflies don their evening light.
It's a party 'neath the boughs,
With nature taking all the bows.

Verdant Luminosity

In fields of emerald, sheep conspire,
To start a game of "dodge the wire."
Cabbages laugh, and peas play ball,
As mushrooms gather for a brawl.

Lettuce slides down humus hills,
While root vegetables perfect their drills.
Bees in hats make quite a buzz,
While broccoli stirs all the fuzz.

Midnight's Verdant Whisper

In the dark, a leaf began to giggle,
A frog nearby let out a wiggle.
The crickets took a front-row seat,
To nature's strange but funny beat.

With fireflies trying to dance and sway,
They stumbled and flew the wrong way.
The moonlight chuckled, a bright old chap,
As branches tangled in a leafy clap.

A raccoon wore a hat made of ferns,
Claiming the night, its victory turns.
It shrugged and slipped on dew like ice,
Turning the forest into a paradise.

Who knew at night, with leaves so bright,
The woods could giggle, what a delight!
Each shadow danced and twirled with glee,
A nighttime party for all to see.

Enchanted Leaves

A squirrel in a coat of leafy flare,
Taught the trees how to do a hair flare.
They giggled as they rustled along,
Swaying to the beats of a silly song.

The acorn boss, with its tiny crown,
Declared that all must gather 'round.
"Let's throw a bash!" it squealed with glee,
"Bring your twigs, make them dance with me!"

The branches bowed to the funky beat,
While mushrooms stomped on little feet.
A hedgehog spun with sass and strife,
Declaring it the party of the life.

As laughter echoed through the night,
The forest woke, a funny sight.
Leaves tittered, with joy they swayed,
In this enchanted, leafy parade.

Glistening Canopy

Under stars, the leaves do shine,
Dancing like they've had too much wine.
A branch waved hello; a vine did yawn,
While chipmunks sang till the break of dawn.

They played a game of peek-a-boo,
Letting the moonlight take a view.
"I spotted you!" the shadows cried,
As all the creatures tried to hide.

The glowing buds joined in the fun,
"Let's start a race! Ready, set, run!"
But tangled roots won the prize instead,
As laughter filled the air, widespread.

So if you wander where the leaves gleam,
You'll find a place where giggles beam.
A canopy that shines so bright,
Holds secret laughs and pure delight.

Verdant Dreams

In the garden, whispers float and swirl,
Where daffodils twirl in a bright twirl.
Petunias wear a funny face,
Chasing butterflies in a silly race.

A dandelion shared its fluffy crown,
Boasting of its wish-granting renown.
The tulips snickered, "What a front!
We're the real stars, we've got the stunt!"

The little bugs had a fancy ball,
In petals soft where they could sprawl.
With crickets playing the trumpet high,
They laughed beneath the playful sky.

So if you dream of a leafy place,
Join the blooms in this parade of grace.
Where verdant dreams come to frolic and play,
With every note, they chase worries away.

Twilight's Green Embrace

In twilight's soft embrace, oh what a sight,
Frogs start a chorus, singing with delight.
A raccoon in a top hat, with flair so grand,
Twirls round a tree, like a woodland band.

Fireflies dance wildly, with sparks of glee,
While squirrels hold a dance-off, just wait and see!
The owls critique the moves, feathers all ruffled,
As bunnies jump in, their tails all snuffled.

The raccoon now juggles, acorns in a row,
While hedgehogs critique his move with a "Whoa!"
Nature's laughter rings in the starry delight,
As twilight's green embrace turns funny tonight.

Harmony of the Lush

In the midst of the woods, so dense and bright,
A gopher wearing glasses saw a curious sight.
A caterpillar played a tune on a leaf,
While ants formed a band, strumming with belief.

A parrot clouded the chorus, voice ever bold,
Said, "Buddies, let's sing, let's do what we're told!"
But the snails were so slow, they forgot the beat,
And ended up dancing on everyone's feet.

Beetles brought snacks, served them with flair,
While ladybugs roamed, spreading laughter everywhere.
The harmony of the lush was never a bore,
With giggles and grins, they just wanted more!

Emerald Tendrils of Light

Emerald tendrils in the night do sway,
With mushrooms as lamps, where critters play.
A chameleon tried to blend, what a fuss,
Stuck in a flower! Oh, the vibrant plus!

A fox in a tutu, dancing with might,
Twisted and twirled in the shimmering light.
The rabbits all giggled, waving their paws,
While the raccoons snapped selfies with 'no flaws.'

Frogs in a line, for the limbo they bent,
While fireflies forecasted the funny event.
Each shimmer a chuckle, each blink a tease,
Emerald tendrils lit the laughter with ease.

Misty Forest Illumination

In the misty woods, where shadows play,
Owls in top hats gathered for a soirée.
A dance of the shadows, with moonlight so bright,
Brought rabbits and deer out for a fun night.

The mushrooms stood tall, like cheerful hosts,
While squirrels challenged each other to toast.
"Let's raise a acorn!" one did proclaim,
"Best dancer tonight, gets to claim the fame!"

A hedgehog spun wildly, stuck with some zest,
Then tripped on a twig—oh, whoops! What a mess!
Still laughter erupted, it filled through the trees,
In the misty forest, where all felt at ease.

Unseen Light of the Woodland

In the woods, frogs dance and prance,
They argue over who gets to glance,
A luminous flash from a pumpkin patch,
As squirrels applaud with a loud 'Hatch!'

Moss wears a hat made of shiny dew,
While owls crack jokes on what's wise to do,
The trees chuckle with a rustling cheer,
As mushrooms giggle, 'We have no fear!'

Emotive Flora

Petunias gossip, I swear it's true,
While daisies wink like they've got a clue,
A rose tells tales of a bee's wild trip,
As his zingy dance gives potions their zip.

The violets wear socks, striped and bright,
While daisies debate if it's day or night,
And cacti whisper secrets real fast,
"Hurry up, that flower hasn't passed!"

Silhouettes of Vermilion Ferns

Ferns wear shades, oh what a sight,
Dancing together, feeling so right,
They laugh at the shadows, twist and shout,
While dragonflies zoom around like a scout.

Each leaf is a lark with stories to tell,
Flirting with sunlight, playing so well,
With whispers of green, they plot and scheme,
'To outshine the bushes, that's our big dream!'

Passionate Green Dreams

Grass blades dream of a wild, fun race,
While twigs form a band, drums keep the pace,
Lilies yell, 'We'll steal the show!'
As crickets take bets on who'll win the flow.

In tall tales spun by vines hanging low,
Chasing the winds that giggle and blow,
'Spin faster!' they cheer; 'Lose the old blur!'
As earthworms cheer them, 'C'mon, let's stir!'

Glistening Garden Secrets

In a garden where gnomes wear hats so bright,
Marigolds gossip under the moonlight.
Sunflowers sway as if sharing a jest,
While bees laugh at the flowers' silly quest.

A squirrel's dance makes the hedgehog snort,
He spins and twirls, a playful sport.
The daisies giggle, their petals a-flutter,
As worms play hopscotch through mud and butter.

With fairies in tutus painting on leaves,
They spill their secrets just like thieves.
And if you listen, whispers abound,
In this lively patch where joy can be found.

Ethereal Emerald

In a land where the plants wear emerald shoes,
The snails are slow, but they don't seem to lose.
Crickets play chess on the lily pad throne,
While frogs sing ballads in a grumpy tone.

A thousand shades of green in the air,
Foxes are prancing without a care.
The chuckles of mushrooms are heard all around,
In this whimsical space where laughter is found.

With dragonflies zooming like tiny race cars,
And toads sharing gossip beneath the stars.
Every blade of grass seems to join in delight,
In this silly realm where odd dreams take flight.

Moonlit Meadow

In a moonlit meadow where shadows play tricks,
The rabbits in costumes do acrobatic kicks.
Owls trade secrets while sipping on tea,
As fireflies giggle with unmuffled glee.

The daisies compete for funniest hat,
While crickets all preach on the art of a chat.
The funny old cat lies in the tall grass,
Dreaming of mice that are swift as they pass.

Each laugh turns to light, as stars twinkle bright,
The night hums with mirth, oh what a delight!
In this whimsy-filled world where silliness grows,
Nature's own comedy, everybody knows!

Rebirth in Radiance

In a world where the flowers can tickle your toes,
They giggle outright, as laughter bestows.
Bouncing back happily after the rain,
The bushes join in for the jesting campaign.

A butterfly sips from a cup made of dew,
And tells the sunflowers, "Have you heard the news?"
The trees sway and shimmy, their branches in time,
As whispers of joy weave a rhythm and rhyme.

In this sprightly parade of whimsical sight,
Even the rocks dance with all of their might.
A toast with the petals—come join us, we cheer!
In this realm of rebirth, let's spread the good cheer!

Off the Vine

A pumpkin donned a party hat,
It danced upon the vine, just like that.
Tomatoes tried to roll with glee,
While cucumbers laughed with a gurgling spree.

The corn was doing the twist, oh so fine,
With carrots cheering, 'Come on, sunshine!'
The peppers threw confetti all around,
As the harvest party shook the ground.

The squash was feeling quite the groove,
While radishes jived and started to move.
The garden burst with laughter and cheer,
As each vegetable raised a pint of beer.

With vines a-twirling and petals all bright,
They partied hard into the night.
At dawn, they snored in a veggie heap,
Dreaming of the fun, so sweet and deep.

Glow of the Enchanted Woods

In woods where mushrooms wear tiny shoes,
The fireflies hold a disco, don't snooze!
With twinkling lights all around the trees,
The branches swayed to a breezy tease.

Squirrels spun like little ballerinas,
While owls hooted out funky arenas.
The raccoons shimmied, slick and so sly,
Chasing shadows as time ticked by.

A fox with shades danced by the stream,
Creating a splash like a woodland dream.
The night was filled with giggles and grins,
As every creature joined in for wins.

With each glow, the laughter grew loud,
Nature's party, so lively and proud.
As dawn crept in, they settled to rest,
With tales of fun, they were truly blessed.

Neon Nurture

In a garden where colors pop and play,
Roses wore shades like it's a runway.
Daisies flipped hair, having a blast,
As the daisies winked, their friends laughed fast.

Veggies in tutus did the cha-cha,
While sunflowers stretched, saying "Oh la la!"
Cucumbers rocked shades, looking so cool,
In this garden, they broke every rule.

Potatoes juggled, what a delight!
While peas painted rainbows, oh what a sight!
The corn began to rap, what a scene,
While carrots fueled laughter with playful beans.

Underneath the cheerful blue sky above,
Nature shared its playful love.
In neon hues, they twirled around,
In a garden where joy knows no bounds.

Light Between the Leaves

Under the trees where squirrels convene,
Sunbeams dance in a silly routine.
Acorns giggle, rolling on down,
While leaves sway to the merry sound.

Bumblebees buzz with a cheerful tune,
Spreading pollen with a sunny swoon.
The ferns giggle, tickled by light,
As shadows play hide and seek at night.

A frog plays the banjo by the creek,
As crickets chime in, week after week.
The butterflies flit, a colorful parade,
In this leafy party, none are afraid.

As moonlight shines through the foliage green,
The woods become a whimsical scene.
With each little laugh, the night feels bright,
A jolly gathering, pure delight.

Secrets of the Sylvan Light

In the woods where critters play,
Frogs wear hats made out of hay.
Squirrels dance in a goofy trot,
Chasing shadows that look quite hot.

Mice throw parties on a big log,
While ants serve tea, dressed like a frog.
They giggle under twinkling beams,
Sharing secrets and silly dreams.

A rabbit trips on a sneaky vine,
Falls into laughter, and feels just fine.
With mushrooms talking in funny tones,
They share wild tales of their wayward drones.

Every leaf whispers a silly jest,
Nature's humor, simply the_best!
In this forest of joy and delight,
Strange things happen in the soft light.

Enchantment Under the Leaves.

Beneath the branches, oh what a sight,
A hedgehog wearing a gown so bright.
The raccoons are hosting a poke ball game,
With mushrooms cheering, calling their names.

Squirrels compete in a nutty drum,
While crickets' chirps turn into a hum.
A dance-off starts, all creatures arrive,
With a glow that surely keeps them alive.

A sleepy owl gives a hilarious shout,
"Who needs an alarm? Just wiggle it out!"
The laughter ripples, a twinkling sound,
As fireflies spin and whirl all around.

The fun continues, oh what a scene,
Beneath all those leaves, life's a routine!
From dusk to dawn, each giggle a tease,
In their magical world, it's all just a breeze.

Emerald Radiance

Glowing leaves with secrets bright,
A party under the starry night.
Frogs wear bow ties, the mice in shoes,
Telling tales that you'd never choose.

Fireflies play tag with a clumsy bee,
While a snail dances with remarkable glee.
A raccoon juggles and starts to trip,
Drawing chuckles from the nearby critters' hip.

A toadstool throne for a tiny queen,
Her crown made of sauntering green beans.
With a flick of her wrist, she calls for a feast,
"Bring the nuts, we're starting at least!"

The laughter drifts like a gentle tune,
Under the watch of a glowing moon.
In this forest, silliness is prime,
Emerald radiance, a laugh every time.

Luminous Ferns

In the shade where ferns start to play,
A lizard struts in a dapper way.
With sunglasses on, he's looking grand,
While grasshoppers clap with a band.

Frogs croon tunes, in quirky styles,
While moles pop out, flashing their smiles.
A dance so wild, all twist and twirl,
While a chipmunk sings to a nearby girl.

A wise old tree starts telling jokes,
Getting giggles from all the folks.
In a flash, they gather, bright and enthusiastic,
Turning each moment just a bit fantastic.

So if you wander where the ferns grow tall,
Listen closely, you'll hear it all.
In this laughter fest, things won't get stern,
With luminous joy, oh the lessons we learn!

Whispering Vines

In the garden, plants conspire,
They giggle low, never tire.
Twisted leaves with gossip sly,
Telling tales as birds fly by.

Parrots perched, they mock the breeze,
While worms debate how to tease.
With tiny leaves that flutter and wave,
It's a party down in the grave!

Squirrels dance on branches high,
Challenging frogs, oh my, oh my!
Beetles waltz with ants in jeans,
The wild's a stage, bursting seams!

So come along, join the fun,
Wiggle and giggle under the sun.
In this place where critters blend,
Nature's laughter will never end.

Shimmering Sustainability

Eco-buddies in a row,
Tiptoeing softly, hat in tow.
Reusable bags swing like kites,
While compost bins throw wild invites.

Laughter bubbles from the stream,
Fish wearing hats, what a dream!
They flip and flop with glee and pride,
As turtles glide, they run and hide.

Bees toss pollen like confetti,
Bouncing here, oh so petty.
Thrifting trinkets, what a chest!
Each find's a treasure, nature's jest!

Join the fun, say cheers to trees,
Dance with flowers in the breeze.
Together we'll save the day,
In this kooky, green ballet!

Radiant Wilderness

In the wild, where critters play,
A squirrel holds a nut like clay.
Hummingbirds buzz in a race,
While raccoons wear a mask and brace.

Branches sway, with foxes snickering,
Mice in capes, their tails flickering.
The mossy floor becomes a stage,
As plants whisper jokes from page to page.

Dancing ferns and laughing trees,
Sway their limbs with greatest ease.
In this nook of vibrant cheer,
Nature's punchlines ring so clear!

So gather 'round, enjoy the view,
The wilds know just what to do.
With humor woven in each nook,
Let's laugh together, take a look!

Celadon Fantasies

In a field of bright, sweet dreams,
Daisies giggle, or so it seems.
A groundhog juggles clovers high,
While butterflies whisper, 'Oh my!'

Grasshoppers bounce, a lively crowd,
Sharing jokes, they laugh out loud.
With sunbeams dancing on each blade,
Nature's humor is well displayed!

The clouds wear hats, puffy and round,
While shadows play, tumbling on the ground.
Tulips chuckle, bowing low,
In this space where whimsy flows.

So hop along, embrace the fun,
Join the laughter, everyone!
In this vibrant, silly spree,
Life's better in our fantasy!

Green Reveries Unveiled

In the garden, snails take flight,
Wings of joy, a silly sight.
Hop and skip, the frogs conspire,
Joining in the leafy choir.

Caterpillars dance on leaves,
Wearing hats made from the eves.
Chasing shadows, they're quite spry,
While bees buzz loudly, oh my, oh my!

Mice wearing shorts, what a team,
Planning schemes, they laugh and beam.
Every weed a jester's grin,
In this garden, fun begins!

With crickets cracking silly puns,
And squirrels prancing, oh what fun!
In this patch of vibrant hue,
Laughter sprouts, as laughter do!

Soft Emerald Embrace

A beetle rolls a tiny ball,
While daisies giggle, 'What a brawl!'
Worms in tuxedos do their twist,
In this dance, none can resist.

The hedgehogs wear their prickly shades,
Sunbathing by the leafy glades.
A riot of fun, both small and tall,
In emerald hues, they have a ball.

A tender leaf drapes over hedges,
While grasshoppers leap from the ledges.
Chasing the sun with nimble feet,
Join the laughter, oh what a treat!

In this embrace that feels so bright,
Nature blooms with sheer delight.
Every grin and giggle shares,
The joy found in these funny airs!

Glow Beyond the Leaves

By the pond, a gnome in cheer,
Sips on tea, with a little sneer.
Fish jump up, wearing funny hats,
While turtles laugh, oh, hoot like bats!

Chasing fireflies in the night,
Ghostly glowworms, oh what a sight!
Jumping jacks on lily pads,
Making jokes, they're all so mad!

The owls wink with a sly, sly gaze,
In the darkness, they love to raise
Puns about the moon so high,
Underneath the starlit sky.

Toadstools draped in fairy lights,
Hosting parties, oh what delights!
With every chuckle, heartbeats race,
Nature hums, a jovial place!

Cavern of Luminous Growth

In a burrow where shrooms bloom bright,
Mice throw raves each day and night.
With disco balls spun from dew,
They shake their tails, oh what a view!

Badgers don their sunglasses cool,
Hosting parties, making rules.
While bunnies stumble, sweet and spry,
Hopping 'round, oh my, oh my!

In this cavern, laughter leaps,
Jokes exchanged as daylight weeps.
Every shiver shows a grin,
Nature's giggles draw us in.

Even roots are tapping feet,
Becoming part of this grand beat.
With every laugh, the lights will gleam,
In this kingdom of funny dreams!

Traces of Vibrant Growth

In the garden there's a pest,
Dancing with a bug on its chest.
They twirl in weeds, oh what a sight,
Plant party's on, all night, all night!

But wait, here comes a loud old snail,
With a trumpet made of a cabbage's veil.
He honks and toots, it's quite a show,
As daisies clap in the breezy flow!

A frog in a hat hops with glee,
Singing nonsense to the bumblebee.
Mice groove on bikes, small and spry,
Underneath the starry pie-in-the-sky!

And just when you think it's all absurd,
A worm stands up, it's truly heard.
"Let's rock this soil and shake this bed,
Nature's groove is spinning ahead!"

Elemental Green Light

A pickle danced beneath the moon,
With a tutu made of a flower's bloom.
It spun and twirled, a veggie delight,
Making the celery laugh in fright!

Potatoes, wearing vibrant shoes,
Join in the fun to shake off their blues.
They shuffle left, they jiggle right,
While onions stand guard, oh what a sight!

A mischievous carrot plays a prank,
Dressed as a pirate, giving a yank.
He robs the salad, an awkward feat,
And lettuce shouts, "That was our treat!"

The broccoli stands with arms all crossed,
"Who threw the peas? Oh, we are lost!"
Yet, laughter grows, weeds join the fray,
In the moonlit garden, they sway and play!

Awakening of the Leafy Realm

The lily pads wore fancy dresses,
While frogs played peek-a-boo with their guesses.
They leapt and hopped to syncopate,
Beneath the sun, it's never too late!

A duck quacked jokes with a shy old tree,
"Why did the leaf fall? To be free!"
They chuckled and snorted, with joy so keen,
In the wildest patch of vibrant green.

A hedgehog in glasses, reading a page,
Told tales of snails with dreams to engage.
"I once was a knight with armor of moss,
But lost my way, now I'm just the boss!"

As shadows grew long and the sun waved goodnight,
Fireflies suited up, ready for flight.
They twinkled and winked in the fading glow,
"Join our gathering, let the stories flow!"

Elixir of the Emerald Forest

In the woods, a potion was brewing,
Made from giggles and leaves, all pursuing.
A squirrel with glasses checked every clue,
Mixing mischief with drops of dew.

The mushrooms threw a big bash,
Gathering to dance with a noble sash.
A raccoon played DJ, shameless and proud,
With beats so catchy, it drew a crowd!

Bunnies volunteered for a muffin bake,
"Fluffy and fresh, we'll do what it takes!"
They stirred and hopped, flour flew everywhere,
While the hedgehogs baked, without a care.

As night cloaked the green with stars up high,
The animals cheered, "Oh my, oh my!"
For in the forest, with joy and delight,
The elixir of laughter lit up the night!

www.ingramcontent.com/pod-product-compliance
Lightning Source LLC
Chambersburg PA
CBHW070305120526
44590CB00017B/2563